Keep L.O.V.E. Present:
Tidbits for Youth

by Naim S. Muslim

Balboa Press books may be ordered through booksellers or by contacting:

Balboa Press
A Division of Hay House
1663 Liberty Drive
Bloomington, IN 47403
www.balboapress.com
1 (877) 407-4847

ISBN: 978-1-4525-1852-7 (sc)
ISBN: 978-1-4525-1853-4 (e)

Library of Congress Control Number: 2014912439

Print information available on the last page.

Balboa Press rev. date: 3/16/2015

BALBOA.
PRESS
A DIVISION OF HAY HOUSE

ACKNOWLEDGMENTS

KEEP L.O.V.E. PRESENT TID-BITS IS AN ESSENTIAL ADDITION TO THE MENU FOR "CHANGE AGENTS" WHO ENGAGE INDIVIDUALS WHO HAVE CHOSEN THE PATH OF L.O.V.E. AS A FOUNDATIONAL DIRECTION OF BEING. IT IS THE PERFECT "APPETIZER" TO OPEN CONVERSATION... AN EXCELLENT "ENTRÉE" AS THE MAIN COURSE OF CONVERSATION ... OR THE PERFECT "DESSERT" FOR ENDING A CONVERSATION OR GROUP; IT WILL LEAVE THE READER LONGING TO RE-ENGAGE FOR ANOTHER SERVING. THE "MILLENNIAL REMIX" OF THE ALPHABET ... KEEP L.O.V.E. PRESENT TID-BITS BRING A WHOLE NEW EXPERIENCE TO AFFIRMATIONS, CONVERSATION AND DAILY ACTIONS OF SELF-ACTUALIZATION AND L.O.V.E.. EACH PAGE LEAVES YOU "HUNGRY" FOR AN ADDITIONAL SERVING ... SO ... "BON APPETITE" OF KEEP L.O.V.E. PRESENT TID-BITS!

KAREN BARNETT, DIRECTOR OF THE YOUTH TO YOUTH PROGRAM, BRIDGETON, NJ

WOW WOW WOW!!! FROM THE FIRST PAGE UNTIL THE LAST, MY HEART SMILED, LAUGHED AND CELEBRATED. KLP TIDBITS, IS AN AMAZING BOOK THAT OFFERS KEYS ABOUT L.O.V.E. THAT INSPIRES ONE'S LIFE. THIS IS A MUST HAVE FOR EVERYONE.

JACQUELINE ROZIER, MARKET MATRIX 4 MILLIONAIRES

REFLECTIONS ON NAIM S. MUSLIM:
I HAVE HAD THE HONOR TO WORK WITH "BROTHER" NAIM S. MUSLIM OVER THE COURSE OF THE PAST 12 YEARS. THROUGH THAT TIME WE HAVE GROWN IN OUR MISSION AND SPIRIT TOGETHER TO BE COMRADES IN ARMS. I AM CONVINCED HE WILL TRANSFORM SOCIAL INSTITUTIONS, COMMUNITIES AND EDUCATIONAL EXPERIENCES FOR CHILDREN AND ADULTS THROUGH HIS KEEP L.O.V.E. PRESENT MOVEMENT. HIS WORK IS AUTHENTIC AND SPEAKS FOR ITSELF CREATED FROM A PLACE OF PASSION, INTEGRITY, HUMILITY, KNOWLEDGE, AND L.O.V.E.. I AM EXCITED TO BE PART OF THIS JOURNEY WITH HIM AND VALUE THE PRESENCE HE SERVES IN MY LIFE AND THE IMPACT HE HAS HAD UPON ME. I AM MY BROTHER'S KEEPER AND NAIM S. MUSLIM IS MY BROTHER. MY HAT GOES OFF TO YOU MY FRIEND, YOUR WORK IS YOUR PASSION AND WITH THAT IT WILL BE YOUR LEGACY!

DR. JEFFREY ADAMS, PRINCIPAL OF WALNUT ST SCHOOL, WOODBURY, NJ

A NOTE TO THE PARENTS AND CAREGIVERS OF OUR CHILDREN.

A QUESTION WAS ONCE SHARED AND ASKED OF ME THAT OPENED MY BEING UP TO A BROADER REALITY CONCERNING CHILDREN AROUND THE WORLD. I WAS MOVED TO TAKE A REAL GOOD LOOK AT MYSELF AND THE ROLE THAT WE, THE CAREGIVERS, PLAY IN THE NURTURING, GUIDING, TEACHING, INSPIRING, MOTIVATING AND DEMONSTRATING WHAT L.O.V.E. IS TO OUR YOUTH.

THE MAJESTIC POWER OF THIS QUESTION INSPIRED ME TO BECOME MORE AWARE OF WHAT WAS REALLY BEING ASKED. IT WAS AS THOUGH SOMEONE COUNTED TO THREE, SNAPPED THEIR FINGERS AND SAID TO ME WAKE UP, SNAP OUT OF IT. WE ARE THE SPECIAL EFFECTS IN THE LIVES OF OUR CHILDREN AROUND THE WORLD AND YOU ARE NEEDED.

I WAS AMAZED AT THE POWER OF THIS QUESTION. HOW IT DIMINISHED LAYERS OF MY "I THOUGHT I UNDERSTOOD" AND SPAWNED ENLIGHTENMENT OF SIMPLE TRUTH.

THIS WAS THE MOST HEARTFELT QUESTION I EVER HEARD. IT CUT TO THE CHASE, GOT RIGHT TO THE POINT AND LEFT NO ROOM FOR MENTAL GYMNASTICS, POLITICAL JARGON OR RELIGIOUS JUDGEMENT. IT STOPS EVERYBODY IN THEIR TRACKS AND PUTS ALL OF US WHO ARE LISTENING IN THE "NOW".

"NOW" IS THE CALL. OUR CHILDREN ARE OUR "NOW". "NOW" IS THEIR BIRTHRIGHT. "NOW" IS ALL IT IS. EVERYTHING THAT HAPPENS, HAPPENS IN THE "NOW"; THEREFORE, "NOW" ALLOW ME TO INTRODUCE TO YOU AN INSPIRING AND REVOLUTIONARY ANTHOLOGY ENTITLED:
"KEEP L.O.V.E. PRESENT TIDBITS" A POSITIVE CONTRIBUTION TO THE LIVES OF OUR CHILDREN AND THEIR FAMILIES AROUND THE WORLD "NOW".

WE ARE OUR CHILDREN. WE NEED THEM. WE ARE THEIR BIRTHRIGHT AND THEY ARE OUR RESPONSIBILITY TO L.O.V.E.. CONSIDER THE SIMPLE, YET PROFOUND STORIES IN THIS MASTERPIECE AS ANOTHER RESOURCE AVAILABLE TO SUPPORT US IN CULTIVATING, SOCIALIZING AND GUIDING OUR CHILDREN.

AS I REMIND MYSELF, I ENCOURAGE YOU TO REMAIN INSPIRED FOR OUR CHILDREN AND SPEND QUALITY TIME WITH THEM. WE ARE WHAT THEY DESIRE MOST "L.O.V.E.".

THE QUESTION
HOW ARE THE CHILDREN?

FROM THE KEYPER OF KLP, NAIM S MUSLIM

Hi! I am the Keyper of KLP. My friends, the Lve's, call me Lucid. They say I express myself clearly and I am easy to understand. I thought that was nice of them. My friends and I are so excited about you reading this book. Before I go any further, allow me to share with you that KLP stands for KEEP L.O.V.E. PRESENT. One of It's meanings is Busy At Being You — listening and following your authentic heart. The messages that we want to share with you are called Tidbits, which have one main goal and that is to support you in having fun with your life by learning about the wonderful message made available to you by my friends, the Lves, in this book. To the right of this page is the four letter construct "L.O.V.E.." Remember this construct as you read through this book. The goal of this message is to let you know that you are loved. ENJOY!

KLP TIDBITS ARE SHORT CONVERSATIONS ABOUT VALUABLE IDEAS THAT TEACH, REMIND AND CULTIVATE HOW UNIQUE YOU ARE. THE DOTS BETWEEN THE LETTERS IN THE WORD LOVE REPRESENT THE DETAILS ABOUT L.O.V.E. MANY TIMES OVERLOOKED. IN THIS PRESENTATION, THE DETAILS EMPHASIZED ARE:

INSPIRATION, MOTIVATION, STIMULATION AND DETERMINATION.
KLP TIDBITS ENCOURAGE THE GENIUS WITHIN.

KLP TIDBITS ARE THE BOMB, MEANING GOOD.

TIDBITS ARE A MUST...

WE KNOW YOU, THE READER, WILL SEE THE VALUE IN THESE TIDBITS AS WE DO AND HOLD THEM CLOSE TO YOUR HEART FOR "KEEPS".

IMPORTANT NOTE FOR THE SUPPORTING ADULT. ON PAGE 42 THERE IS AN INTERACTIVE GUIDE AVAILABLE THAT CAN BE USED TO ASSIST IN STIMULATING CONVERSATION WITH THE READER.

THE FLOW

CALL ME,
LABEL OF VITAL ENERGY

Why?
Because I want
you
to know
that I define
myself.

Like you, I was born
unique, smart,
intelligent, happy, kind,
energetic and full of fun.
I am special.

Those are
the labels
that I like.

Like
me, don't allow
anyone to label
you negatively.
Label
yourself: GREAT
PERSON.

HEY! I'M

LANE OF VITAL ENERGY

YOU SEE, EVERYONE IS BORN TO DO SOMETHING SPECIAL IN THE WORLD.

YOU, ME, MOM, DAD, AUNTS, UNCLES, NEIGHBORS, FRIENDS, EVERYBODY.

THE KEY IS TO AND DON'T GET DISTRACTED.

STAY FOCUSED AND KEEP DOING YOUR WORK.

CHECK OUT MY NAME:
⌊ANGUAGE Of Vital Energy

JUST LIKE ME, YOU LEARNED YOUR ABC'S.

HERE IS HOW YOU ARE TO USE THEM:

TO TALK ABOUT L.O.V.E., CREATE L.O.V.E. AND TO SHARE L.O.V.E.

LET'S PRACTICE. REPEAT AFTER ME. I L.O.V.E. ME AND YOU.

I AM THE
L.A.W. OF VITAL ENERGY

I AM KNOWN AS THE
LEAP OF VITAL ENERGY

HERE'S WHY.

I WAS TELLING MY TWIN "LAUGHTER", WHO YOU MET EARLIER THAT I AM TAKING ANOTHER LEAP OF FAITH TO START MY THIRD BUSINESS.

HE LAUGHED AND SAID THIS IS THE THIRD TIME YOU DID THIS. YOU HAVE PLENTY OF HEART. I GUESS THAT'S WHY YOU ARE SO SUCCESSFUL.

I SMILED AND SAID, "LIVE YOUR DREAM! LIVE YOUR DREAM!"

LEARNER OF VITAL ENERGY

YOU WILL MEET MY BIG BROTHER. HIS NAME IS LION. HE IS SO SMART. HE'S FEROCIOUS ABOUT LEARNING.

HE SAYS, "I'M BRAVE AND STRONG LIKE A LION." EVERYDAY HE REMINDS ME TO DO WELL IN SCHOOL.

HE'S SO POSITIVE. HE'S A GOOD ROLE MODEL.

RESPECTFULLY, I AM KNOWN AS:

LEGENDS OF VITAL ENERGY

KNOW ME AS:

LETTERS OF VITAL ENERGY

THERE ARE TWENTY SIX LETTERS IN THE ALPHABET. THE 12TH LETTER OF THE ALPHABET IS THE LETTER "L". THE WORD LOVE STARTS WITH THE LETTER "L".

THAT MAKES THE LETTER "L" A SPECIAL LETTER.

HERE ARE SOME OTHER SPECIAL WORDS THAT START WITH THE LETTER "L".

LABEL
LABORER
LADY
LANE
LANGUAGE
LAUGHTER
LAW
LAWYER
LEADER
LEAP
LEARNER
LEGACY
LEGENDS
LESSONS
LETTERS
LIBATION
LIBERATION
LIBERTY
LIFE
LIFESTYLE
LIGHT
LIMITS
LINEAGE
LINKED
LION
LISTENING
LITERATURE
LOOK
LORD
LOTS
LONGEVITY
LOYALTY
LUCID

I CELEBRATE MY NAME,

 **LIBERATION OF VITAL ENERGY**

BE LIKE ME. FEEL FREE TO TALK ABOUT L.O.V.E. ANYTIME.

L.O.V.E. COMES FROM THE HEART, SO SPEAK FROM THE HEART.

PEOPLE L.O.V.E. TO TALK ABOUT L.O.V.E. BECAUSE L.O.V.E. IS GOOD.

OH YEAH! HERE I AM,

IFESTYLE OF VITAL ENERGY

LIFE IS FUN, ESPECIALLY BEING AROUND FAMILY AND FRIENDS WHO L.-O.-V.-E. AND TEACH ME ABOUT ALL KINDS OF FUN THINGS.

THINK ABOUT THIS.....

BEING GOOD, LOOKING GOOD, CHOOSING GOOD, ACTING GOOD, BEHAVING GOOD, TALKING GOOD, THINKING GOOD, LISTENING GOOD. PARENTS ARE GOOD, TEACHERS ARE GOOD, ELDERS ARE GOOD AND YOUR FRIENDS ARE GOOD. WOW! GOOD IS EVERYWHERE.

IN MY HEART I'M THINKING, "THANK YOU" FOR THE GOOD LIFE AND GOOD PEOPLE. THAT'S WHY LIFE FOR ME IS SO MUCH FUN. YEAH!

CARING ME,

ifting OF Vital Energy

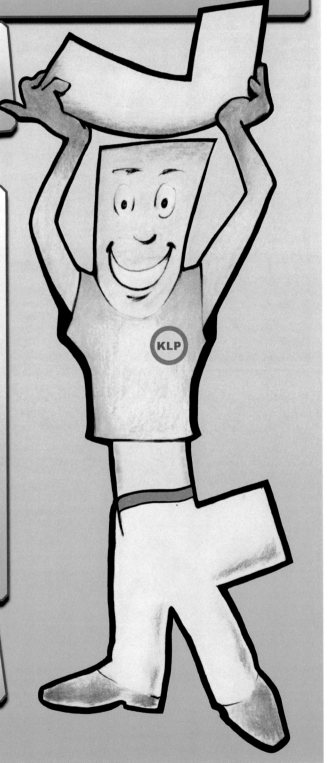

YOU MET THE TWINS LAUGHTER AND LEAP ALREADY. LETTERS AND I ARE TWINS ALSO. LETTERS HAD A NICE TIDBIT. CHECK OUT MINE.

A KIND WORD, A HELPING HAND, SHARING A GIFT, RECEIVING A GIFT. HELLO, HAVE A GOOD DAY. COME IN, HAVE A SEAT, HAVE A BITE TO EAT, WOULD YOU LIKE MORE? YOU ARE INTELLIGENT, YOU LOOK NICE TODAY. HI! MY NAME IS, WHAT'S YOURS? MAY I ASSIST YOU WITH THAT? LET ME DO THAT, THAT COLOR LOOKS NICE ON YOU, THANK YOU VERY MUCH, HAVE A GREAT DAY. DID YOU REST WELL? I L.O.V.E. YOU, I L.O.V.E. YOU BACK, THANK YOU FOR THE RIDE. BLESS YOU, YOU DROPPED THIS, YOU ARE SO KIND, ETC.

THESE ARE ACTS OF L.O.V.E. THAT MAKE PEOPLE FEEL GOOD. AND I FEEL GOOD WHEN I DO ANY ONE OF THEM.

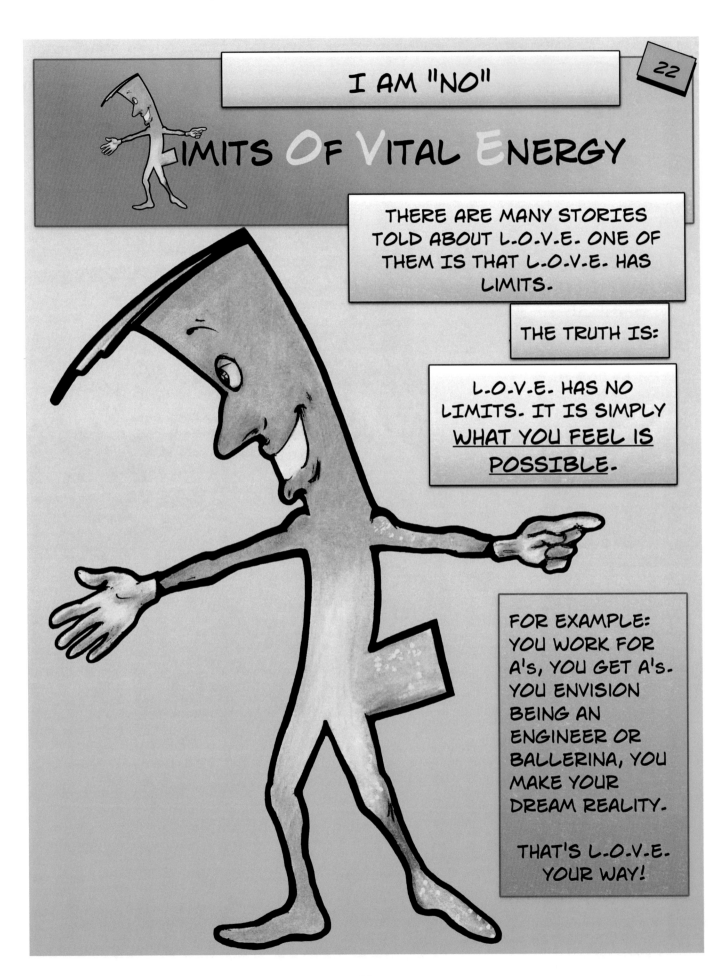

Lineage Of Vital Energy

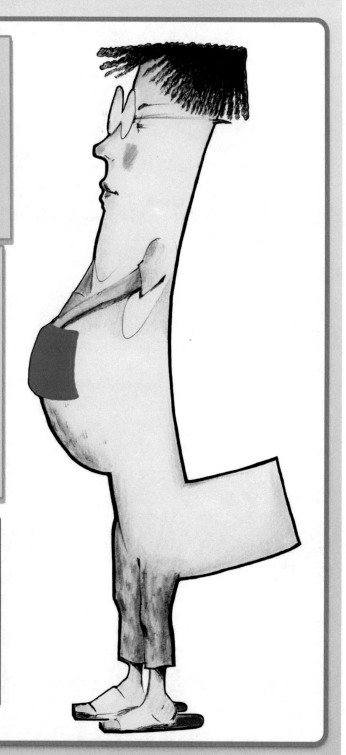

FROM GENERATION TO GENERATION, L.O.V.E. IS PASSED ON. THROUGH L.O.V.E. WE STAY NATURALLY CONNECTED.

LABORER OF VITAL ENERGY SHARES L.O.V.E. ALL THE TIME. I AM PROUD OF HIM. HE'S MY HARD WORKING HUSBAND YOU LEARNED ABOUT EARLIER. I WORRY ABOUT NOTHING.

WE HAVE A BEAUTIFUL FAMILY AND WE ARE GETTING READY TO CELEBRATE OUR NEW ADDITION AND ADD HER TO THE FAMILY TREE.

IPS OF VITAL ENERGY

AS A REPRESENTATIVE OF L.O.V.E., WE TALK ABOUT GOOD THINGS ALL THE TIME.

WE EVEN GREET ONE ANOTHER WITH KLP, WHICH IS SHORT FOR KEEP L.O.V.E. PRESENT. THE RETURN IS L.I.P., WHICH IS SHORT FOR L.O.V.E. IS PRESENT.

L.I.P. WITHOUT THE DOTS ALSO SPELLS THE WORD LIP. THIS MEANS THAT THE ONLY TIME WE SHOULD HAVE A LOT OF "LIP" IS WHEN WE ARE TALKING ABOUT A LOT OF L.O.V.E.

REMEMBER THAT.....!

30

LIVING ON VITAL ENERGY

LIVING IS WONDERFUL ESPECIALLY WHEN YOU MAKE GOOD CHOICES.

REMEMBER THIS! "NO", IS JUST AS IMPORTANT AS "YES".

CHOOSE TO SAY <u>YES</u> TO GOOD THINGS THAT SUPPORT YOU AND <u>NO</u> TO BAD THINGS PERIOD. BE PATIENT AND GOOD THINGS WILL HAPPEN.

OK! OK!

ACCEPT IT! I'M

LONGEVITY OF VITAL ENERGY

29

ALLOW ME YOUR UNDIVIDED ATTENTION. HERE IS SOME VERY IMPORTANT INFORMATION ABOUT L.O.V.E.

L.O.V.E. IS PURE
L.O.V.E. IS UNIVERSAL
L.O.V.E. IS YOURS
L.O.V.E. IS MINE
L.O.V.E. IS FRIENDSHIP
L.O.V.E. IS PLENTY
L.O.V.E. IS CHILDREN
L.O.V.E. IS ABSOLUTE
L.O.V.E. IS EVERLASTING
L.O.V.E. IS CULTURE
L.O.V.E. IS UNDERSTANDING
L.O.V.E. IS PEACEFUL
L.O.V.E. IS FREE
L.O.V.E. IS FAULTLESS
L.O.V.E. IS ABUNDANCE
L.O.V.E. IS CARING
L.O.V.E. IS VIRTUOUS
L.O.V.E. IS DEMONSTRATED
L.O.V.E. IS L.O.V.E.
L.O.V.E. IS YOU
L.O.V.E. IS LIFE
L.O.V.E. IS THIS BOOK
L.O.V.E. IS ....

TO BE CONTINUED....

WITHOUT DOUBT I AM,

Loyalty Of Vital Energy

LYRICS OF VITAL ENERGY

I'M MC

34

SIT BACK AND RELAX FOR A COUPLE MINUTES. I HAVE A POEM I WANT TO RECITE FOR YOU.

STOP IN THE NAME OF L.O.V.E.,
EVERYDAY GIVE YOUR FAMILY EMBERS A GREAT BIG HUG;
MAKE GOOD CHOICES AND KEEP A SMILE ON YOUR FACE,
UPPORT ONE ANOTHER AND KEEP L.O.V.E. IN THIS PLACE;
AMILY IS NUMBER ONE WE KNOW THIS IS TRUTH,
STICK CLOSE TO ONE ANOTHER LET L.O.V.E. BE OUR PROOF.

1. LABEL YOURSELF. WHAT WOULD IT BE?

2. WHAT DO YOU WORK HARD AT THAT MAKES YOU FEEL GOOD ABOUT YOURSELF?

3. WHAT ELSE WOULD YOU ADD AND WHY?

4. NAME SOME THINGS THAT CAUSE YOU TO LOSE YOUR FOCUS.

5. CREATE YOUR OWN PERSONAL "I L.O.V.E. YOU" PHRASE.

6. LIST THREE WORDS DESCRIBING YOUR EMOTIONS WHEN LAUGHING.

7. SHARE TWO MORE LOVING SAYINGS THAT WILL MAKE PEOPLE SMILE.

8. WHAT WOULD YOU LIKE TO WORK HARD AT BEING?

9. WHAT MAKES YOU A LEADER?

10. DO YOU UNDERSTAND LEAP OF FAITH?

11. WHO REMINDS YOU TO DO GOOD IN SCHOOL AND WHAT MAKES THAT SPECIAL?

12. HOW CAN WE WORK BETTER TOGETHER?

13. DEFINE THE WORD DEBUNK AND USE IT IN A SENTENCE.

14. SHARE WITH ME WHAT THIS TIDBIT MEANS TO YOU?

15. GIVE ME SOME OTHER POSITIVE WORDS STARTING WITH "L".

16. LETS SAY WE ARE DOING A LIBATION, WHOSE NAME WOULD YOU CALL OUT?

17. WHAT IS KLP TO YOU?

18. DO YOU KNOW WHAT IS MEANT BY THE TERM SELF-EXPRESSED?

19. DESCRIBE HOW YOU HAVE FUN WITH THOSE WHO L.O.V.E. YOU.

20. LET'S DO AN ACT OF L.O.V.E. TOGETHER! WHAT DO YOU THINK?

21. LIGHT FUNCTIONS IN MANY WAYS. NAME TWO?

22. THINK ABOUT YOUR POSSIBILITIES. DON'T LIMIT YOURSELF.

23. DO YOU KNOW WHAT A FAMILY TREE IS?

24. GIVE SOME OTHERS WAYS PEOPLE SHARE LIFE.

25. DISCUSS YOUR LIKES/DISLIKES ABOUT SCHOOL.

26. L.I.P. STANDS FOR WHAT?

27. WHAT MAKES LISTENING NECESSARY?

28. WHAT MAKES SAYING "NO" IMPORTANT?

29. WHAT ELSE CAN L.O.V.E. BE TO YOU? COMPLETE THE STATEMENT. L.O.V.E. IS _____

30. WHETHER YOU ARE MALE OR FEMALE, WHAT ARE SOME OF THE THINGS YOU WILL DO TO STAY BEAUTIFUL?

31. WHO MADE ALL THINGS?

32. NAME A DIFFICULT EXPERIENCE THAT TAUGHT YOU A POSITIVE LESSON.

33. WHAT MAKES L.O.V.E. NUMBER ONE TO YOU?

34. THINK ABOUT THE TIDBITS YOU HAVE READ. WRITE A POEM DESCRIBING WHAT YOU'VE LEARNED ABOUT KLP.

WRITE YOUR OWN TIDBIT

LEARNER OF VITAL ENERGY

PUT YOUR LOVE ONES FIRST AND DON'T EXPECT TO BE TREATED GOOD WHEN YOU'RE TREATING EVERYONE ELSE BADLY

BRANDON GREENE, GRADE 3

LOVE COMES FIRST AND KINDNESS TO OTHERS. IF SOMEONE IS BEING BULLIED YOU SHOULD SPEAK UP FOR THEM

JACOB BENHEY, GRADE 3

CARE ABOUT OTHERS, KEEP ONE ANOTHER SAFE, SHOW RESPECT TO ALL PEOPLE

KEELI MCCARTHY, GRADE 4

I THINK KLP IS LIKE A BALANCE BEAM. YOU GIVE LOVE AND KEEP THE BALANCE EVEN. IT MEANS TO REALLY KEEP GIVING LOVE AND GETTING LOVE AND KEEPING YOUR BEAM BALANCED. MY GOAL IS TO KEEP GIVING LOVE AND ACCEPTING LOVE TO KEEP MY BEAM BALANCED

AMBER MONTESINOIS, GRADE 5

HELP AND CARE FOR EACH OTHER AND WHEN SOMEONE GETS HURT, YOU HELP THEM

AMELIA ALZZAN, GRADE 3

KEEP LOVE IN YOUR HEART

OMAR BROWN JR., GRADE 3

KEEP OTHERS FEELINGS SAFE AND LOVED AND TO BE NICE.

NIANNI PIERCE, GRADE 5

RESPECT OTHER PEOPLE EVEN WHEN THEY'RE MEAN TO YOU AND TREAT PEOPLE AS NICELY AS YOU CAN

ZACHERY LEEDS, GRADE 3

LOVE WHERE YOU ARE

ANONYMOUS YOUTH, GRADE 4

TO ALWAYS LOVE AND KEEP LOVE PRESENT IN YOUR HEART AND IF YOU HAVE A ARGUMENT, FIX IT WITH LOVE

NICOLE BOGRIS, GRADE 5

BE HELPFUL AND KIND. HELP PEOPLE FIND THINGS THAT ARE LOST. LISTEN TO OUR TEACHER

MAGGIE MCCUMBER, GRADE 2

FROM THE FAMILY TREE OF KLP

KEEP LOVE PRESENT MEANS KEEP LOVE PRESENT, WHETHER YOU ARE HURT OR HAPPY AND TO NOT ALLOW PEOPLE TO MAKE YOU SOMEBODY YOU'RE NOT.

NAIM MURRELL, AGE 16

KLP MEANS TO LOVE MY OMN SELF.

ELIJAH MURRELL, AGE 4

KLP TO ME, OF COURSE IS KEEPING LOVE PRESENT. THE BASICS OF KEEPING LOVE PRESENT IS ALWAYS HAVING LOVE, AND NOT JUST FOR OTHERS, BUT FOR YOURSELF AND OTHER LIVING THINGS ON THE PLANET. KLP IS LOVING PEOPLE WHO DON'T LIKE YOU OR PICKING UP TRASH AROUND YOUR NEIGHBORHOOD WITHOUT BEING TOLD. KLP IS JUST HAVING A CONSTANT GLOW OF LOVE, THAT PEOPLE CAN SEE, HEAR, AND FEEL.

DEMYYA WELCH, AGE 16

KLP—IT MEANS TO ALWAYS KEEP LOVE PRESENT AROUND YOU AND ALIVE WHEREVER YOU GO. AND TO KEEP LOVE PRESENT EVEN WHEN THINGS ARE NOT GOING GOOD AND YOU JUST FEEL DOWN. JUST KEEP L-O-V-E- PRESENT ALL AROUND YOU AT ALL TIMES AND THEN YOU WILL BE HAPPY BECAUSE YOU WILL BE KEEPING LOVE PRESENT!!

KIYAH WELCH, AGE 13

KLP IS LOVE, IT'S GREAT AND IT'S RESPECT.

NYAH MURRELL, AGE 11

KLP MEANS TO KLP WHEREVER YOU GO, EVEN IN THE FUTURE. ALSO, KEEP L-O-V-E- PRESENT INSIDE YOU. THE MORE LOVE YOU HAVE, THE MORE IT WILL SHOW AND THEN IT WILL SPREAD. SO ONE DAY THE WHOLE WORLD WILL KEEP LOVE PRESENT.

KAZI WELCH, AGE 11

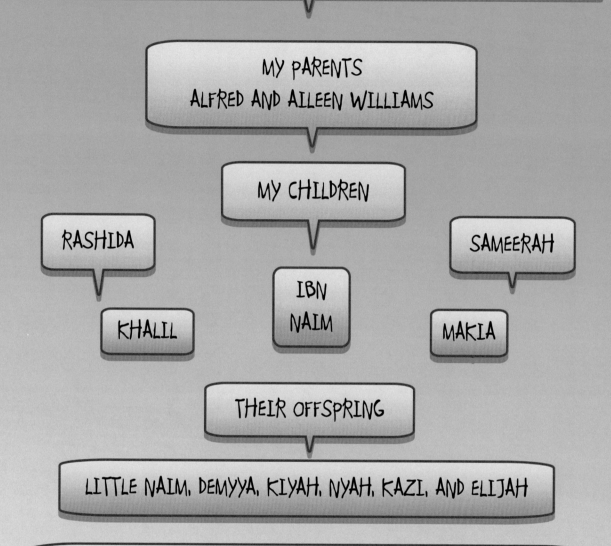

THIS WORK IS DEDICATED TO MY PARENTS, MY CHILDREN AND THEIR OFFSPRING.

MY PARENTS
ALFRED AND AILEEN WILLIAMS

MY CHILDREN

RASHIDA

SAMEERAH

IBN NAIM

KHALIL

MAKIA

THEIR OFFSPRING

LITTLE NAIM, DEMYYA, KIYAH, NYAH, KAZI, AND ELIJAH

A SPECIAL THANKS TO
RASHIDA MURRELL AND BIATA UTTERBACH FOR EDITING and
DENNIS JONES AND CASBAR SALAAM FOR THEIR CREATIVE SUPPORT.

ALSO, A VERY HEARTFELT THANK YOU TO
ELDER CHARLES ROBINSON FOR HIS UNTIRING
MENTORING, GUIDANCE, WISDOM AND L.O.V.E.

AND DON'T FORGET YOUR DAUGHTERS

Follow NAIM at:

TWITTER.COM/WORDDESIGNER

CAUSES.COM/KEEP LOVE PRESENT

LINKEDIN.COM/NAIM S. MUSLIM

FACEBACK.COM/ KEEPLOVEPRESENT

Printed in the United States
By Bookmasters